All it takes is an hour

𝒜wareness and Contentment

Rod Willner

This book is dedicated to my son Bodhi.

Contents

	Page
Introduction	1
Contentment	4
Awareness	10
Putting it all together	18
Dealing with Negativity	24
From where I sit – a personal note	28
Conclusion	29

Introduction

Hi! I hope you're comfortable where ever you are. Got a cuppa? This should only take about an hour, so lets begin.

Firstly, I would like to say that if you are reading this little book of mine, thank you for picking it up and I really do hope that you enjoy it. Secondly, I would like to give you some of my reasons for writing this.

I believe that we should look for wisdom from many different sources and take what we need from each one and discard what we don't. No one book or piece of advice can possibly tell us exactly what we need to know for the rest of our lives. We are constantly growing and forever changing so the words of wisdom that we seek should continue to inspire us throughout our lives. Also we are all very different as individuals. There are no two people alike in this big world of ours, so wisdom should also differ for each person.

There are many self-help books available today, I have read a lot of them and have learned a lot and I would encourage you to try them yourself. There are some great reads around! That said, I haven't written this book to try to place myself in the same league as some of these writers but to hopefully add a little of my own.

Lastly I would like to say that I have learned a lot whilst writing this little book. I would also like to thank all the forces that were involved in putting this together. So let's go!

I'm going to get straight to the point and tell you only need to know, understand and put into practice, the meaning of two simple words, in order to be happy in your life.

The first word...

Contentment

This is a very powerful and simple word with an all-encompassing meaning. So what does it mean to be content? And what am I content with? There are easy answers for these types of questions, so lets take a look.

The good thing about contentment is that it is a feeling, or emotion, that can be felt across all aspects of your life. Contentment can be coupled to relationships, family and friends, finance, career and lifestyle. Literally anything that you do, love, enjoy, experience etc. Understanding its meaning unveils a powerful tool for building happiness. To know the word and to understand it is easy, but to put it into practice, well that's a little bit harder. But the rewards are fulfilling and life long, and the best part is that you get to control every single aspect of it!

So, how can we be content? Well, it's time to look inward and ask some serious questions, and provide some honest answers.

Take a look at all aspects of your life and paint a mental picture of the things that you are not content with. Be it a relationship, where you live, your looks, your career etc. If it helps, write it all down. Now ask yourself, why you are not content in these areas. What is it that makes you feel this way?

When thinking about things that we're not content with, there's often something else that creeps into our thoughts… and that's comparison. We compare ourselves to just about everything and everyone. Why do we do this? Well, the answer is that it gives us perspective. But is it a good way to get perspective? Should we avoid comparison altogether? No, definitely not, but we should change the way we compare. This is what I believe to be the best way of turning discontentment into contentment. Lets explore this.

Some would say to avoid comparison at all costs and that it is a destroyer of dreams. "You are one and you are unique", they say. "You are not the same as anyone else on this planet". "Who you are and what you do is truly original". Although these words are true, this is not necessarily the best advice. A different approach is needed.

When we hear people say "Never compare" they are usually referring to comparing with people that are better looking, are more successful, have more money, better relationships etc. And by doing this, we inevitability feel worse off. But, what if we were to compare ourselves to someone that is less fortunate, someone that does not have money, good relationships etc. If we did that, would it not paint a better picture for ourselves? Would we not have more appreciation for what we already have? And compassion for them, might I add.

One of my favourite sayings has always been "compared to what". A comparison can either be a very positive experience, or a very negative one depending on what we actually compare too! So, compare all you like, but be content with what you have, and work on what you have. Because there is always someone worse off than you! Ok, lets keep moving. Don't let your cuppa get cold!

The next word...

Awareness

I think the phenomenon of awareness is more powerful than anything else. In fact, I could have written this book entirely on awareness alone!

So what is awareness, and why is it so important? Awareness is your key. It is what unlocks your feelings and your emotions and sets you free. It has the power to give you a good day, or a bad one, a happy life, or a sad one. Awareness is all encompassing, and we have to understand this to be able to use it to our advantage.

There are different things that we should be aware of, and these things provide different advantages for us. For example, if we focus on being aware of ourselves, our own feelings and emotions, we will in time, begin to understand ourselves better, which in turn will give us a better quality of life. That's a no-brainer right? Isn't that what every self-help guru talks about? But wait there's more! What about the awareness of others? How does that affect us?

When we become aware of others, we notice that the things we say and the things that we do (our actions) have an impact on others. We can then quickly and easily work out what provides a positive reaction, and also what provides a negative one.

We can then adjust how we speak and act around others in order to bring about more pleasant interactions with those around us. This is like changing the future, or influencing destiny, because you can literally change your day, your week, even your life by being aware of how your words and actions affect others. And more importantly, how it affects you. It really is that easy!

A few years ago I put this to the test with a young man that I used to manage. He agreed to partake in an experiment with me, and it went something like this. Every day for a week, we were to go out for lunch and look around the shops. We would interact with as many people as we possibly could, in the cafes, shops and even in the street.

It was agreed that I would do what I normally do. Smile at everyone I interact with, speak nicely, ask how his or her day is, get to know as many of the shopkeepers on a first name basis that I could and generally create a nice vibe between myself and the people that I interacted with.

My employee on the other hand, had completely different instructions to follow. I asked him to speak directly to the people that he interacted with, only asking for what he wanted or needed, never smiling or saying thank you, hello or goodbye. Basically, he was to remain stoic and unemotional. He did this (very well I might add) for the week during our experiment.

The following Monday we went to lunch to talk about what we had experienced the previous week. For me, it was a good week full of nice experiences. I met lots of new people, and knew most of them by name, and they knew mine. They remembered my favourite coffee, what I liked for lunch, I even got a free slice of cake! They smiled at me and said hello each day.

To sum it up, my week was quite a pleasurable experience.

My friend on the other hand, had something completely different to report. He didn't have a good week at all! He had received bad service from people. Some of them had stopped smiling at him and spoke to him quite abruptly. One young lady in a café even tried to ignore him and not serve him. In summary, he was not real happy about his experiences during the week.

So it's pretty obvious to see what went on here. I created a happy environment for myself using no more effort than he, just by treating others differently and being aware of how my words and actions influenced those people. He only achieved feelings of being miserable, and probably influenced those he interacted with to feel something similar.

He never believed that he could influence his future, his state of mind, his happiness, let alone influence others. He does now!

Be aware of what you say and do. Understand how your actions and words affect others. It's just like cause and effect, action and reaction, or you can call it Karma if you're more comfortable with that term. It's not that hard; in fact it's really simple… if you try.

This is where the fun stuff begins. It is also where things get a little difficult. But as I mentioned earlier, the rewards are life long.

Awareness and contentment... we all know these words, and we understand them. But how do these two things connect? How do we couple awareness with contentment? The answer to this is actually quite easy... Be aware of what makes you content! Make it your mantra, your positive affirmation!

I am aware of what makes me content
I am aware of what makes me content
I am aware of what makes me content

This statement might seem too simple, and you'd be right in thinking so. But if put into practise, it can become the key for you to find happiness. Have a think about this. Put this book down for 5 mins. Better still, go and make another cuppa!

Back again ... got your cuppa? Good, lets continue.

All you have to do is become aware of the things that make you feel content. The things you say, your actions, others around you, your relationships, your career, your friends, your children, your location, your age, your looks etc. Being aware of what makes you content can put all of these things into perspective.

Put contentment into your thoughts. Contemplate it is often as you can during the course of your day. Focus on it, and focus on everything that you have in your life that brings you contentment and ultimately makes you happy.

This should become a state of mind, a kind of conditioning, that will bring upon happiness. And remember that all I'm talking about here is a change of thought, a shift in thinking, so to speak. This does not require any additional effort. Just a change in the way you look at things.

Pretty soon, this awareness will start to change the way you act, what you say, and even the decisions that you make. You'll begin to understand the connection with your words and actions, being aware of the effects on others and your awareness of this phenomenon.

Over time, this will become automatic. It will occur without you even thinking about it. Sure, you'll stop and notice it occasionally, but ultimately this will happen without you knowing, and without effort. It will continue to go back and forth until you find a balance that does nothing but sustain your happy state of mind.

You'll be walking around with a silly grin on your face, perplexing those that fix their eyes upon your expression. Making them wonder just what you've been up too, to be smiling like that. Oh, and wouldn't they like to know!

You'll feel a constant bliss and complete contentment (there's that word again). You'll radiate nothing but confidence. Your family and friends will notice a change and people will ask what you've done, or what are you doing to be so happy. You'll start to feel more alive than you ever have before. You'll be more confident, empowering and strong. Your relationships will grow stronger and deeper. You'll make better decisions, achieve more, and ultimately be more successful.

All of this can, and will, happen. But it is not something that is going to happen quickly. It took me a few years to get to the point where my awareness drives almost everything that I do. I was a bit slow on the uptake. However, you may grasp this concept and put it into practise very quickly, and then begin to notice the changes. However long it takes for you to get this working, just trust that it will be worth it; I can personally vouch for this.

Dealing with Negativity

How do we deal with negativity and negative people? It's an unfortunate reality that some people like to put others down when they are trying to improve themselves or better themselves. It is also inevitable that you will act kindly and speak nicely to some that may not reciprocate.

It is important to note that not everyone that you smile at, speak nicely too and treat kindly is going to react in a positive way. Lets face it; some people seem to prefer to just be grumpy all day! However this is about you and the changes that you can make to enrich your life, so focus on the people that react kindly. As for the grumpy people… just smile at them more, it makes them even grumpier. But hey, don't tell them I said that!

As far as other people's opinions are concerned, the most important thing that I can tell you is this. Don't worry about what people say or think! Just like that old saying "What people think of YOU is none of YOUR business". It's easy to say but hard to do right?

Indeed, but remember that this is your life. This is your trip; it's your ride. You (yes you!) get the final say in everything concerning you. It's only a choice, and it's a choice that you can make starting today!

From where I sit — a personal note

You've probably already worked out by reading this little book of mine that awareness and contentment is pretty important to me, particularly awareness. This has always been at the forefront of my thinking, and as my close friends and family would probably tell you, it's something that I've been babbling on about for years! However, they would also tell you, that the proof is in the pudding! Because they have been able to observe how I manage to sail through life relatively unscathed.

The things that I write about in this little book are put into practice in my life, every single day. I live and breathe these principles, because I know that they work! I also hope that they work for you.

Conclusion

It is my wholehearted wish that you can take something from this little book of mine and use it to help you be a happier person. If you already are a happy person, perhaps you can help a family member or friend to be happier in their life. Just as the movie says, "Pay it forward".

So that's the end of our short time together. I do hope that our exchange has been beneficial. Exchange you say? Yes, writing this little book has been a learning experience for me too.

As I leave you now, I have just one thought in my mind … I wonder what we can talk about next time?

You ponder that, and I'll put the kettle on.

About Rod Willner

Rod's love of words began at the young age of 13 when he started writing poetry. At around the same age, he also discovered his passion for music. It wasn't long before the inevitable happened, and his poems began turning into songs.

His passion for words is still as strong as it was when he began to write all those years ago, and it remains a very integral part of his life.

Copyright © 2018 Rod Willner

First published in Australia in 2018
by Karen McDermott

karenmcdermott.com.au

All rights reserved. No part of this book may be used or reproduced by any means, graphic, electronic, or mechanical, including photocopying, recording, taping or by any information storage retrieval system without the written permission of the copyright owner except in the case of brief quotations embodied in critical articles and reviews.

All the information, techniques, skills and concepts contained within this publication are of the nature of general comment only and are not in any way recommended as individual advice. The intent is to offer a variety of information to provide a wider range of choices now and in the future, recognizing that we all have widely diverse circumstances and viewpoints. Should any reader choose to make use of the information contained herein, this is their choice and the contributors, and companies authors and publishers do not assume any responsibilities whatsoever under any condition or circumstances. It is recommended that the reader obtain their own independent advice.

ISBN: 978-0-6481906-8-4 (sc)

Series of 8 books by Rod Willner

karenmcdermott.com.au

www.ingramcontent.com/pod-product-compliance
Lightning Source LLC
Chambersburg PA
CBHW062106290426
44110CB00022B/2733